Young Dancers

Purnell

SBN 361 04516 6
Copyright © 1981 Purnell & Sons Limited,
Published 1981 by Purnell Books, Berkshire House, Queen Street,
Maidenhead, Berkshire
Made and printed in Great Britain by Purnell & Sons Limited,
Paulton (Bristol) and London

One of the essential requirements of a ballet studio is a full length mirror in which students can observe their positions and correct any faults.

Purnell's book for

If I were a young person and wanted to become a ballet dancer, I know there are certain preparations I would want to be wise enough to make.

I think, first, I would be determined that I wanted more than anything else in the world to become a dancer. I say that because without that determination one would be lost. The hours and hours of training and study and then rehearsal need a strong will besides a strong body. People are often amazed when I compare a dancer to an athlete, but it's true. We both must always keep in perfect condition and if I were a student I'd know that means plenty of early hours and to be always in top training form.

I would study the great dancers of today and yesterday. The techniques of the Russian and Italian ballet methods, the performances of the ballet companies that visit your town or city. All these will give you inspiration.

I would give much of my spare time to learning music, listening and studying so as to further my knowledge of this art that is so much a part of dancing.

I would find an excellent ballet teacher. I would convey to the teacher my ardent sincerity and desire to work. I would try and absorb and learn all this teacher could teach me and I would continue studying with the best teachers available, preparing myself for the examinations and auditions that would lead to employment with a ballet company.

I would work hard to develop style and grace and then, after being told by someone who knew when I was ready, I would appear at every ballet company audition and dance and dance and work to be accepted in the Corps de Ballet, where I could closely watch the great stars and develop my own dancing.

These are the things I would do if I were a young dancer anxious to become a great dancer.

How I Fell in Love with Ballet

ave you ever dreamed of becoming a ballet dancer? If you have, you might be attending ballet classes already, or perhaps you are planning to join a class near your home. Maybe you just enjoy reading about ballet and want to know more about it.

My name is Anne. I am learning to dance and I would like to tell you all about myself, my ambitions and how wonderful my life is as a ballet student. I shall also tell you about ballet schools, about the steps and techniques I am learning in class with my friends, about examinations to be taken and all the other things you will want to know about ballet and ballet dancers.

First, though, I should tell you how I fell in love with ballet and how it came to be so important to me. I had been going to dancing classes for a while at the local church hall and really enjoyed the thrill of moving in time with music, as well as making new friends with other girls and boys who shared my excitement and enthusiasm for this new discovery of ours.

One day, after an especially hard and tiring lesson, our teacher told us that we had been very good with our practice and were getting along well, so as a special treat the whole class was to go to a Schools' Matinee performance of "Giselle" at the London Coliseum. We were all tremendously excited as most of us, myself included, had never seen a live ballet performance before.

But there was better yet to come: two of the greatest ever Russian stars, Natalia Makarova and Mikhail Baryshnikov, were to dance the leading roles. We could hardly believe our good fortune and counted each day to the performance eagerly. Finally the magic day dawned. We were taken to the theatre by coach and led into the auditorium where I took my seat amidst the excited chatter of my friends.

Suddenly the house lights dimmed and went out, music began to flow from the orchestra and as the curtain rose I felt myself being transported into a fantastic and beautiful world.

When the dancers took their first bows and the curtain fell for the last time I cried, partly with sorrow for Giselle and her Albrecht, but mostly because I had never

In the wings just before curtain-up, Marilyn Burr removes the knitted leg warmers which help prevent pulling muscles before they are properly warmed.

Left: Hilda Morales and Warren Conover of the American Ballet Theatre in the light-hearted and ever popular Pas de Deux of Giselle's friends in Act I of the ballet.

before seen anything so beautiful and moving as the dancing Sylphs floating so gracefully across the stage in their long white dresses. Now that it was all over I knew that more than anything else in the world I wanted to join these wonderful fairy-tale characters and dance like them.

At our next lesson, when I had come down to earth a

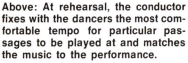

Above: At rehearsal, the conductor fixes with the dancers the most comfortable tempo for particular passages to be played at and matches the music to the performance.

Above centre: Giselle, danced by Natalia Makarova, is crowned Queen of the Wine Harvest and is hailed by the villagers and her beloved Loys, danced by Mikhail Baryshnikov.

Right: In Act II Giselle joins the ranks of the Wilis in the forest, spirits of girls who have died from broken hearts before their wedding day, led by the awesome Myrtha, who exacts vengeance on all men for their faithlessness.

Far right: Natalia Makarova in her most famous role as the happy Giselle, as yet unaware that Loys has deceived her and is, in reality, Prince Albrecht and already betrothed to another.

Top right: At the end of a ballet performance, the cast receive a great ovation from the audience and the principal dancers and stars are presented with bouquets of flowers.

11

Right: The choreographer, who creates the ballet, is always there at the Dress Rehearsal in order to make the few finishing touches to his work. Here the famous Vaslav Orlikowsky is working with the two principal characters from his ballet Peer Gynt.

Far right: The dressing rooms at opera houses are strange and wonderful places where ordinary people enter but from which fairy tale characters emerge, after the skilled application of make-up and costume.

Below right: Like any other, the ballet orchestra has to rehearse new works and adaptations of old ones until every member is familiar with them.

Below: The great dancers Nadia Nerina and Attilio Labis rehearsing a Pas de Deux from Swan Lake at the Royal Ballet School.

12

bit, our teacher told us about all the hard work, backstage preparation and rehearsal that has to be done before the public see the complete and polished performance. It all seemed terribly difficult and complicated but it was fascinating and it made me realise that all those magical characters that I had admired so much were, after all, real people just like me and that if I really tried I might one day be lucky enough to enter their world.

I made up my mind then and there and nervously but full of hope I went home and told my parents that I wanted to become a ballet dancer.

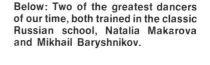

Below: Two of the greatest dancers of our time, both trained in the classic Russian school, Natalia Makarova and Mikhail Baryshnikov.

The beautiful and ethereal Sylphide floats down on gossamer wings from the window to meet her beloved, James, from the ballet La Sylphide.

Looking Ahead

t first my parents did not take me seriously and thought that it was just a passing phase. This only made me more determined and I threw myself into my dancing classes with renewed enthusiasm. I wanted to dance so much that I practised every new movement over and over again until it was perfect, following all the advice my teacher could give me. At home, I ate, slept and breathed ballet, reading every book I could find in the library on the subject. Mum and Dad soon saw how seriously I was taking my interest and began to encourage it. In class my teacher recognised the change in me and began to take extra notice of what I did. I was delighted when she told me I was showing promise. When I went home and told my parents what she had said they decided to go and see her with me to talk about my possible future in ballet.

One day after class, when I had taken special care to do every position just right, we all had tea together in the canteen and talked about my future. Mum and Dad were anxious to find out about the likely openings and the possible risks involved in a dancing career and, of course, what were my chances of success. Miss Adams told us that there had never before been so much interest in dance. Its tremendous growth in popularity had meant a great increase in the number of professional companies needing trained dancers, therefore opportunities were good. My parents were relieved to hear that conditions and pay had greatly improved in recent years and that it is now possible to earn a very good living from dancing, especially if you progress to soloist or even star position. Of course, the competition for places is high, but the opportunities are not restricted to ballet; a trained dancer can find work in musical theatre, in films, television and international cabaret. Teaching is another possibility for a successful student. In short, the opportunities are there; it all depends on what you make of them. Miss Adams added that I was very lucky because I had one great advantage, I had shown myself to be dedicated and more than anything else, dedication is the key to a successful career. Only this special quality can keep you going through the hard training, the endless

Above: Students at the Arts Educational School learning the dramafic art of mime, "I beseech you".

Below: Some small touring companies are like a big family where everybody lends a hand; the dancers even help paint the scenery.

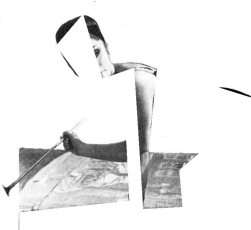

Far right: Not all ballet students become ballerinas, but it's a safe bet that these TV pop dancers have had classical training which forms the basis of all modern dance. Many dancers also work in musicals and shows, and many of our great entertainers have risen from the ranks of the ballet schools.

routine of practice, the physical strain and the aches and pains that form part of a dancer's everyday life and which you must endure in order to be successful.

However, few dancers regret this hard work, as the rewards of success are so great. As for whether or not I had the makings of a dancer, Miss Adams said that I was in good health and was fortunate to have a good physique for a dancer, not too tall and with arms and legs not too long or too short, a good length neck and a strong back. Most important, I had a good sense of discipline in class, and showed a good 'ear' for the music, from which a dancer gets her dramatic inspiration and upon which the whole tempo and form of the performance depends. After hearing all this my parents were a lot happier about my plans and asked Miss Adams what she thought the next step should be if I were to seriously consider a career in dancing.

Above: The growth of interest in ballet in recent years has meant that more and more is being televised or made into films and so has reached a larger audience than ever before.

Right: Students of the Kirov school in Leningrad put into practice their lessons in stage make-up for their school performance. It is important to emphasise the features of the face and in particular the eyes, mouth and cheekbones are accentuated with shadow, lipstick and rouge.

Choosing a School

iss Adams told my parents that if I wanted to pursue a dancing career I would have to go to a proper school. There I would be taught all the subjects that any ordinary schoolgirl would learn, such as mathematics, English and science, but would also take lessons in the dramatic arts including dancing, music and drama. She emphasised that there was no need to worry that my general education would be neglected as the academic standards of these schools are very high. To enter such a school I would have to audition, and the examiners would be looking for a dancer with a suitable physique and promise of success. They would not expect to see a polished performer, only the raw material from which they might make one. Miss Adams thought I stood a very good chance of getting a place.

The only problem remaining was which school to choose. There are quite a number not only in this country, but also abroad. A school in a foreign country is no barrier to the ballet student as ballet has an international language of its own, dating back to the days of the great Sun King, Louis XIV of France, under whose reign the foundations of classical ballet technique were first laid down. In any ballet school in the world the positions and movements are always referred to in French and so a dancer of any nationality can immediately understand instructions. In the great international ballet schools there are many different nationalities all getting along well together and sharing the same enthusiasm for their studies.

Here are some of the world's top schools to consider when making a choice:

The Royal Ballet School:

This school is closely linked to our own great British ballet company, the Royal Ballet, and it is well known throughout the world for its high standards. Young students come from many countries to study here and many great stars have emerged to join not only the Royal Ballet, but most of the world's top ballet companies.

This young student at the Kirov school in Leningrad is doing a few practice pliés to warm up and relax her muscles before class begins. A short time before you wouldn't have been able to tell her apart from any other schoolgirl, chatting with her fellows on her way to class.

Above: Dancing is not the only form of art taught at White Lodge. Painting is encouraged and what the students learn will be put to good use when they have to make scenery for the school performance.

Below: A mixed class at White Lodge, the junior school of the Royal Ballet in Richmond Park.

The school is divided into two parts: the Lower School and the Upper School. The Lower or Junior School is in White Lodge in the heart of the beautiful Richmond Park in London. This started life as a royal hunting lodge for King Henry VIII, but now the great halls and galleries are used as schoolrooms and studios, creating the ballet stars of tomorrow. The students here are aged from eleven to fifteen and once they have reached a certain proficiency the best go into the Upper or Senior School in Talgarth Road, London. This, as well as

being a purpose-built school with light airy studios, is used by the Royal Ballet company as rehearsal studios and often you can see some of the world's greatest choreographers creating new works with top ballet stars in one studio, while in the next students are taking class. The highlight of the year is the school performance which is held at the Royal Opera House, Covent Garden, London, in which the year's best students get a chance to perform in a great theatre. If these students show enough talent they may eventually be lucky enough to gain a place with the Royal Ballet itself; those who do not go to other branches of the performing arts, or even modelling and in all these careers their first-class training is well worthwhile.

The Royal Danish Ballet School:

The Royal Danish Ballet has a great reputation for keeping the traditions and original forms of classical ballet, thanks to two main reasons. The first is that the school has continued without a break since 1748. The second is the brilliance of one man,

21

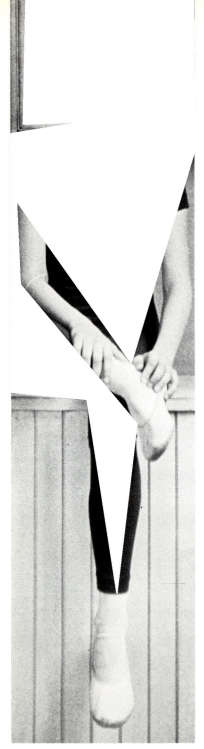

Auguste Bournonville, who became its ballet master in 1829, and under his guidance Danish Ballet reached its peak. Trained by the great Vestris in Paris, he taught the pure French style and through his beautiful choreography created such ballets as La Sylphide and Napoli. The Danes have always loved his talent and to this day the 'Bournonville' style and his ballets form the major part of their repertoire. The school attached to the ballet company is the second oldest in the world. It is housed in the great Royal Theatre in the heart of Copenhagen. Students of this school are taught free of charge from the age of seven until they reach the age of sixteen, when they may enter the company itself. As the Bournonville style relies heavily on brilliant male solos, there are more boys at this school than at some others and there has been a tradition of great male dancers there such as Erik Bruhn, Flemming Flindt, Peter Schaelfuss and Henning Kronstam who is now a director.

Rosella Hightowers School:

The students of Rosella Hightowers School are very lucky, for it is built in one of the most glamorous areas in Europe, Cannes on the French Riviera.

Above: A young girl in the junior class looks on as some of her classmates go through an enchaînement.

Right: Henning Kronstam, world famous dancer with the Royal Danish Ballet and now director of both school and company, takes a master class and gives a student's feet particular attention.

The lucky girls pictured here must surely be the envy of their peers. They are students at the Rosella Hightowers School in Cannes on the sunny Côte d'Azur. Attending school there is almost like being on permanent holiday. However, they still have to follow the very strenuous routine of all ballet students. One added bonus, though, is that because of its very attractive surroundings, leisure facilities and light airy studios, the great stars of the ballet world often go there to take class and rehearse. In this way the girls have the priceless opportunity to study their technique at close quarters.

The Paris Opera school is the oldest established and one of the most respected in the world. It is situated at the heart of the city in the opera house itself. In the labyrinth of studios and classrooms one can find lots of Little Rats. They are not real ones, of course. This is the affectionate nickname given to boys and girls studying there and who will one day graduate to join the ranks of the parent company.

Opened only in 1961, this young, residential school is set in beautiful surroundings with perfect facilities for dancing and is a favourite place for great dancers such as Erik Bruhn and Rudolf Nureyev to come and practise. Rosella was one of the most popular ballerinas in Europe during the 1950's and was noted for her brilliant technique. She is a very good teacher and her students reach high standards. They also have the chance to watch great dancers at class and pick up valuable tips themselves. The students are happy and enthusiastic and Rosella, who both teaches and administers the school is a friend to all her pupils. She also has a troupe which performs at the Casino in Cannes and on tour abroad. After a strenuous class, when the school day is over, some of the students can be seen relaxing on the beach lapped by the blue Mediterranean. No wonder this school is so popular!

Paris Opera: School:

The Paris Opera School or École de Danse de L'Opera was founded in 1713, making it the oldest in the world. Here, within the walls of the Opera House itself, you will find 'Les Petit Rats' (Little Rats), the affectionate nickname given to the young students lucky enough to be enrolled at this famous school. At the Paris Opera School it is not necessary to know how to dance before applying, but you must pass a strict medical examination. Then, after three months of ballet classes every evening, there is a dancing examination and if you are successful you may enter the school proper and choose a 'petite mere' or a 'petit pere' (little mother or father) from the corps de ballet of the company to help you during your training. Throughout the training there are five stages with an examination for each. When there are suitable children's parts in a ballet, the most promising pupils are allowed to perform with the company. Finally, at the age of sixteen you have the opportunity of joining the company as a member of the corps de ballet. If you are good enough you can

progress from there to a 'Coryphees' a leading member of the corps, then to Petits Sujets, then Grands Sujets or soloist; then 'Premier Danseur' or 'Principal' and finally the most important position, 'Danseur Étoile' or the star.

Kirov Opera: School:

When speaking of the major ballet schools a name to remember is that of the Kirov, a school which has produced a string of world famous dancers. Started in 1738 its graduates include such names as Nijinsky, Nijinska, Fokine, Pavlova, Ulanova, Balanchine, Nureyev and Makarova. Indeed, the small school theatre has trained so many of the famous, great ballet dancers that visitors are said to kneel and kiss the stage at this shrine of ballet.

Nowhere is ballet so important as in Russia and

The name Kirov is one to conjure with when talking of schools. Dancers of surpassing excellence continually emerge from the ranks of its students to amaze the world with their athleticism, grace and technique. You begin to understand why when you see the absolute concentration and dedication on the students' faces in class, as they learn from some of the world's greatest teachers the particular Russian style. Once class is over, however, everyone relaxes and the atmosphere of camaraderie is as happy and friendly as in any school.

students of dance are sent from all over the country to the Kirov School in Theatre Street, Leningrad, to train for stardom.

The rules of this school are very strict. First all students must learn Russian, as so many students come from far flung parts of the country where a different dialect, or even language, is spoken. The ballet classes are held by some of the greatest teachers alive, famous ex-dancers passing on their classical skills and knowledge to their pupils and encouraging the talent in them. It is a very happy atmosphere, the students are inspired by what they are taught. Their total dedication shows in the concentration on their faces during class.

The Bush Davies School:

The late Noreen Bush was one of the leading teachers of ballet in Britain. Her whole life was devoted to ballet and after a distinguished dancing career she and ex-pupil, Marjorie Davies, opened the

Bush Davies School in 1939. This residential school is at Charters Towers, East Grinstead, in the Sussex countryside and is one of the best equipped dance schools to be found anywhere, with light, purpose-built studios and modern classrooms for general education. The junior girls sleep in dormitories and are looked after by a matron, while the more senior girls have shared rooms which they decorate with colourful posters or pin-ups of their favourite dancers. The Adeline Genée Theatre which is situated in the grounds is used for school performances, and also as a proper playhouse for the area. Adeline Genée was one of the founders of the Royal Academy of Dancing, and Noreen Bush was one of the first five dancers to pass the Academy's advanced level exams. She later became a friend and colleague of Dame Adeline and eventually named the theatre after her.

You can find out more about ballet schools, scholarships and careers on page 55.

Below: A senior class at work in the light and modern studios of the Bush Davies School, many of whose students graduate to join the top international dance companies.

Life at Ballet School

Mum and Dad wrote to a few of the top schools for detailed information and I waited anxiously each morning to see if the post brought a reply. When the prospectuses started to arrive, we read each of them carefully and discussed which schools I would most like to try and join. The prospectuses were very informative and told us how to apply, explained the dance and drama courses available and standards of general education, together with pictures of the school and grounds. I found it all very exciting, especially the photographs of the schools and students at work in class and in end of term productions.

The schools I liked best were the Arts Educational Schools, one at Tring Park in Hertfordshire, a boarding school for girls, the other at Golden Lane in London, a day school for boys and girls. This is a very famous old school. The main building at the Tring School is a splendid and historic mansion, but there are also beautiful new buildings with light classrooms and studios as well as bedrooms for the middle and senior students. The grounds are particularly attractive and include an indoor swimming pool as well as tennis courts and riding facilities. I could hardly believe that this could be a school at all!

I could tell that my parents were very impressed, not only by the brochure but also by the list of some of the past pupils of the school, dancers such as Antoinette Sibley, Anton Dolin and John Gilpin and actresses like Claire Bloom, Margaret Lockwood and Julie Andrews. As well as dancing, there are lessons in drama, music and art for all the students which ensure a sound basic training in all the theatrical skills. This varied training is invaluable as not every pupil will become a ballerina. Many of the great stars of stage, cinema and television started their careers in the dance class.

After a lot of thought and discussion we finally agreed that this was the school that would suit me best so I wrote to Tring Park asking for an audition. These are held several times a year and to apply you send an application fee, a medical certificate and a small, full-length photograph of yourself in practice clothes.

Above: The school has very well equipped art studios and here an accomplished student demonstrates her prowess at the potter's wheel.

Below: One of the charms of the main building is a concealed door made to look like bookshelves and those not in the know can get quite a surprise as a bevy of girls pop out of nowhere.

Imagine how excited I was when I heard that I had been accepted for audition, but as the great day approached I was very nervous in spite of everyone's encouragement and helpful advice.

Above: Two of the girls from different years having a chat in one of the bedrooms in the newly built additions to Tring Park, where girls can decorate the walls with their favourite posters, not always of dancers.

Centre: Arts Educational girls and boys have a reputation for smartness and are taught always to be well turned out. This quality seems to fit well the many splendid rooms in which classes are given.

Far right: Just before the audition, a candidate carefully and neatly ties the ribbons on her shoes.

Below: Quiet Please! Students at their "O" level art exam. They can draw inspiration from some of their fellows' work adorning the walls.

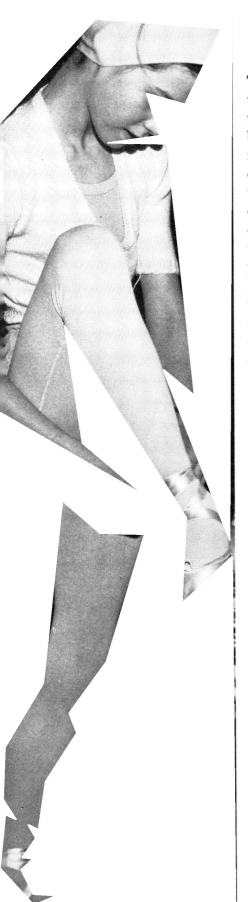

But I knew more than ever that I wanted to join the Tring Park School and my nervousness vanished as I took my place with the other applicants. We were asked to complete short written tests in English and arithmetic but they were not too difficult. Then came the audition itself. One by one we were called in and when my turn came I stepped into the big room and was introduced to the School Principal, Mrs Jack, a very kind person, who explained what I had to do and put me completely at ease. First I had to do some exercises at the barre and then in the centre as demonstrated by a teacher. They were much the same as I had learnt in my dance class. Following this I was given a piece of poetry to recite which I tried to do as slowly, clearly and with as much feeling as possible. I did not sing but played a short piece on the recorder for the examiners. At the end of the audition they all smiled reassuringly and thanked me for attending. I left the room feeling quite pleased with myself. Everything had gone so well.

Back at home, about a week later, the letter for which I had been patiently hoping came. I had been accepted and would be joining the school at the beginning of the following term. Mum and Dad were delighted and I felt on top of the world! I had passed the first big hurdle.

When the school term started, I felt very proud of my smart, new uniform, which marked me as an Arts Educational girl. I found it easy to settle in to the school routine as everybody was so friendly and there was such a happy and relaxed atmosphere. The senior girls helped us find our way around and I soon made a lot of new friends. Our school day was divided in two: half for general subjects such as English, maths, French, history, art and needlework, and the other half for vocational lessons: ballet, modern dance, tap, drama and music, with a break at midday for lunch. In our free time we could swim in the pool, play games in the grounds or just relax with a book from the school library.

All this new activity was rather tiring at first but we soon got used to the daily exercise and the aches and pains quickly vanished as we became more involved in our dancing and made quick progress under the expert instruction of our teachers.

Preparing
for Class

One of the very first things that we all had to learn at our new school was how to prepare for ballet class. The school had sent us a list of clothing and equipment needed and where to buy it, so that we all arrived with the same basic 'kit'. In class we wore a blue leotard over pink knitted tights and white socks. The leotard was made out of stretchy jersey material, which, although close-fitting, allowed the body and arms to move freely. The woollen tights were to keep our leg muscles warm and supple, as attempting ballet exercises before your legs are properly 'warmed up' can lead to pulled muscles or even torn ligaments. Such an injury can weaken a dancer's legs for life.

Our hair was to be kept neatly pinned back from our faces in a bun, so that it would not fly about and flick into our eyes during practice; to keep it in place we wore a wide blue hair band.

On our feet we wore soft leather pumps without any heel for barre and centre work and in these we were only able to go up as far as demi-pointe, with our weight on the front of the foot. Eventually when our feet and legs became stronger and could take the strain, we were allowed to go on to full pointe, right on the tips of the toes, something that every student wants to be able to do.

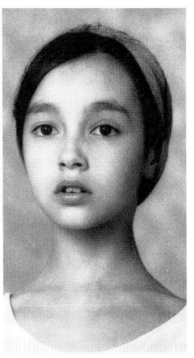

Above: The right way to look for class: smart, clean and hair neatly combed out of the face and secured by a headband.

Below: Senior students at the Royal Ballet School change into pointe shoes before moving on to pointe work.

Above: When you buy a pair of ballet shoes for pointe work it is necessary to darn their toes. This will provide more grip on the floor and will help prevent wear as this point takes the full weight.

Right: Young girls preparing for class at the Kirov school in Leningrad's Theatre Street.

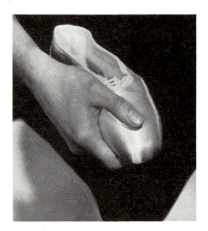

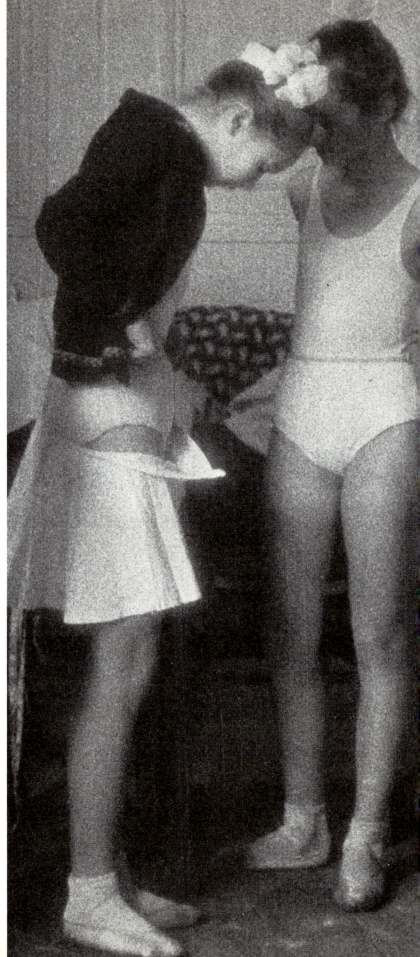

It is a great landmark when you are allowed your first pointe shoes and can begin training to go up on full pointe. Pointe shoes are specially strengthened along the sole and have their tips 'blocked' with glue, to help give more support. Good shoes are essential to a dancer. The pain and damage that a badly fitting or stiff pair of shoes can cause must be avoided at all costs. To make sure that we did not suffer with our feet we were shown how to break in ballet shoes. Like all shoes they are stiff when new and have to be worked in your hands to make the soles more supple and flexible without cracking them. This process may take a little time but it is time well spent in saving you from discomfort and enabling you to concentrate fully on your dancing.

The next lesson to be learnt is how to sew the ribbons on to the shoe. This is something that every dancer must know as it is important to position the ribbons properly to suit yourself. A general guide is that, after folding in the back of the shoe, the ribbons should be sewn on at the fold between back and sides. Once the shoe is on, you tie up the front strings and tuck them out of sight and then go on to tie the ribbons in a special way, tightly but not tight enough to stop ankle movement. The ends of the ribbons must finally be tucked in out of the way.

There is one more thing to learn about pointe shoes, how to darn them. This is done to the toe of the shoe to give it more grip than the slippery satin provides and to help prevent wear on the part which takes the greatest weight. In fact, so much wear occurs that sometimes dancers get through several pairs in one performance!

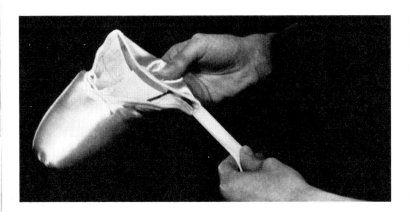

Above: Dancing is all about freedom of movement and it is very important to choose a leotard which gives you this while remaining comfortable and close-fitting to the body. You cannot wear anything restricting if you hope to perform with fluency and grace.

Left: Every dancer learns to sew the ribbons on a shoe herself. It is important to know how to do this because the most comfortable and exact position varies from dancer to dancer. As a guide though they can be sewn at the angle made when folding down the back of the shoe.

37

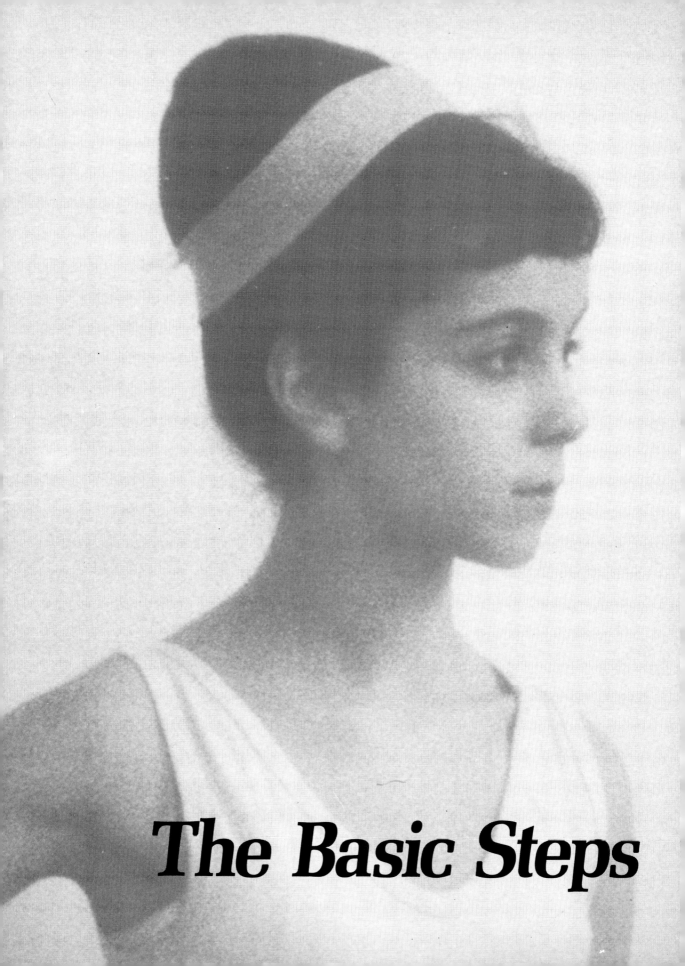

The Basic Steps

nce in class you learn about the importance of 'stance' and 'turn-out' before you can do any exercises. Stance is how to stand correctly. Your hips should be positioned directly over your feet and your back and shoulders should be straight.

Turn-out is the way in which the whole length of the leg is turned outwards and to the sides from the body. Good turn-out is very important. It gives your body a beautiful line, it is the foundation of the five basic positions, and is the starting point for all the movements in classical ballet.

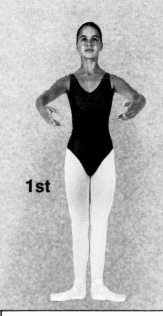

1st

2nd

3rd

4th (open)

4th (crossed)

5th

The 5 basic positions: Always be conscious of your stance and turn-out. Keep your arms relaxed from shoulder to fingertip, never stiff or awkwardly bent, but forming a smooth natural line. This is known as Port de bras (carriage of the arms).

1st position: Heels together, arms held in soft curve to the front.

2nd position: Feet apart (about $1\frac{1}{2}$ times foot length between heels.) Arms held outwards in a gentle unbroken line to middle finger.

3rd position: The heel of one foot is brought to the middle of the other, arms in a combination of 1st and 2nd position.

4th position: Two of these, the first of which is the "open" version. One foot is placed about 24cm (12″) forward from 1st position, with the weight equally divided on both.
In the second "crossed" version, the feet are still parallel and apart but the heel of one is in line with the toe of the other.

5th position: The most difficult to master. The feet are together and parallel, the toe of one foot touching the heel of the other and vice versa. The arms are held upwards in a long gentle arc.

The Barre

Class begins with exercises at the barre. This is a wooden rail on which you lightly rest your hand and use as a support as you go through the preliminary or first exercises. Each exercise is repeated several times on both sides of the body so that there is no uneven strain on the muscles. The series of exercises performed is designed to slowly warm, loosen and strengthen the muscles and joints in the legs so that you can then go on to more difficult and strenuous movements.

Nos. 1+2: Plié in 1st position. Starting from 1st and keeping well turned out, bend the knees and descend smoothly, returning again to the original position.

No. 3: Repeat this exercise in all 5 positions. Pictured is a demi-plié in 2nd position.

Nos. 4.5.6: Battement tendu. Starting from 5th, the foot slides to the front, returns, to the side (à la seconde), returns, to the rear and finally back to 5th position.

No. 7: Battement frappé: The leg from the knee down is kicked outward to the front, then to the side (pictured) and finally to the rear before returning to the starting point with foot flexed.

Nos. 8+9: Fondu: Here to the front and side. This exercise strengthens the legs, readies them for grands battements and trains them to help in jumping and landing smoothly.

Nos. 10+11: Grands Battements: Here to the front and rear. The leg having properly warmed up, now swings as high as possible without unbalancing the posture or supporting leg.

Nos. 12, 13+14: Développé: Here in 2nd position. From the retiré position the leg is slowly extended to its full length and as high as possible, returning to 5th position. Only to be attempted with fully warmed muscles.

No. 15: Développé derrière to arabesque: The leg has been unfolded to the rear and ends in arabesque position.

No. 16: Arabesque penchée: In the arabesque position the body is inclined forward and the leg raised correspondingly higher.

Before proceeding to centre work, which is without the support of the barre and where further strain is put on the muscles and tendons, there are stretching exercises one can perform to loosen and prepare your body even further.

No. 1: Dégagé in éffacé: Dégagé means with extended foot and éffacé means at an angle to the audience with the arm nearest them raised to present a narrowed body aspect.

No. 2: Écarte: The dancer's legs, arms and head are all held in the same plane.

No. 3: 1st Arabesque: Extendded arms and leg.

Nos. 4+5: 2nd Arabesque: First à terre (leg touching ground), then en l'air (leg raised).

Nos. 6+7: 3rd Arabesque a terre, then en l'air.

Nos. 8+9: Attitude croisée à terre derrière: This position is croisé (crossed) because the one leg appears crossed in front of the other and the rear leg is raised and then we reach the full attitude croisée en l'air derrière.

Nos 10+11: Fondu croisé devant: (Devant: to the front) Starting from this position with supporting leg slightly bent, it is then straightened and the other raised into position attitude croisé devant.

No. 12: Retiré: As at barre then

No. 13: Développé devant

Nos. 14+15: Retiré then Dével-
‾‾ á la seconde (2nd posi-

Centre Work

When you have finished at the barre and your muscles are fully warmed up, you can move on to centre practice, which, as its name suggests, takes place in the centre of the classroom. At first it feels strange without the barre as support, but gradually your confidence improves. You learn to enjoy the greater sense of freedom as you progress to difficult movements and eventually your teacher shows you how to link them up into little sequences called 'enchainements'. This is when you begin to feel that you are really making progress and starting to dance.

1   2   3   4   5

6   7   8   9   10

11   12   13   14   15

Jumps

Ballet audiences always enjoy watching the daring leaps of the dancer, who makes them look so graceful and effortless. But such leaps are not easy to do and need many years of hard practice. The jumps that we start with in class are only small ones designed to strengthen and prepare our bodies for the greater ones to follow in later years. It is a marvellous feeling, though, to leap gracefully into the air like a real ballerina!

Below: Every dancer darns her own shoes and sews on her own ribbons. You must make sure that the ribbons are neatly tied and the ends tucked in. When you first start with pointe shoes you begin once more with the basics, only this time on pointe until such time as your feet are stronger and you can tackle more demanding movements.

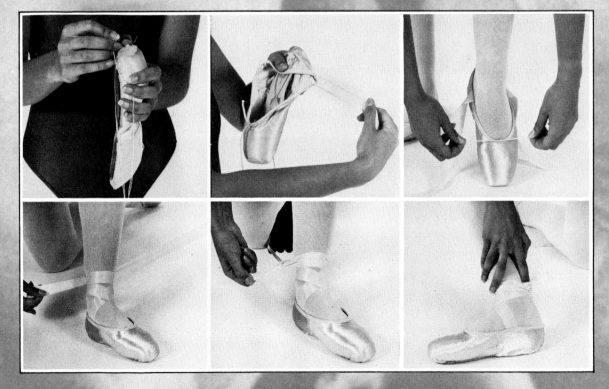

Pointe Work

It is a great day when you are allowed to go on pointe for the first time; it is something that every student longs to do as it is then that you really feel you have achieved the light and graceful style and line of the true ballerina. Pointe work, though, must not be started too early, you must wait until your feet are strong enough to take the strain or they can become deformed and only a qualified teacher will know when you are ready. Warming up exercises are always done first and it is not until these are over that you put on your pointe shoes, making sure that the ribbons are neatly tied and the shoes fit snugly. To begin with, a series of exercises are performed at the barre and then in the centre, gradually strengthening the feet and helping to improve technique until one day, hopefully, dancing on pointes becomes second nature.

Top left: A few simple jumps.

1) Sauté à la seconde: jump from 2nd position.

2) Temps levé: jump upwards from one foot.

3) Jeté en avant: leap forwards.

Below: Some basic positions to practise on pointe. At first you will need the support of the barre.

1) 5th position, with one foot tucked closely behind the other.

2) 2nd position, with heels closer together than in a full 2nd.

3) Crossed 4th.

4) Relevé from 5th position.

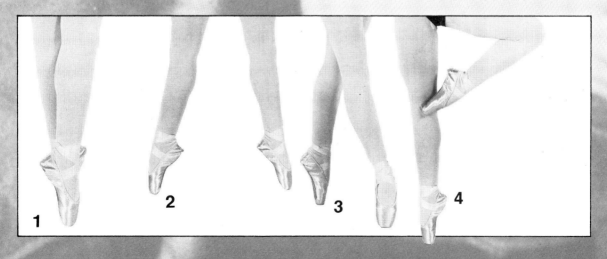

The expert eyes of the examining board assess the performance of the students.

Exam Time

ith ballet, just as with any other subject, there are examinations to be taken and levels of proficiency to be reached. These examinations are only taken when your teacher thinks that you are ready, as different students develop at different rates. There are two sets of examinations to be taken at the Arts Educational, those of the Royal Academy of Dancing which concentrate on ballet, and those of the Imperial Society of Teachers of Dancing which cover ballet, modern dance, national dance and tap. Both the R.A.D. and I.S.T.D. examinations have three levels: Elementary, Intermediate and Advanced. Twelve is about the earliest age for Elementary and then, depending on how well you are doing, Intermediate comes a year to eighteen months later and Advanced after a slightly longer period. The examinations are made up of set exercises at the barre and in the centre as well as enchaînements. Naturally these become more difficult at each level and the standard of technique expected by the expert panel of examiners becomes higher. No matter how good you are, everyone is nervous at the thought of the exams and so you will need to practise extra hard beforehand, but everyone remains friendly and you will all offer encouragement and good luck wishes to each other as you take turns to show your paces.

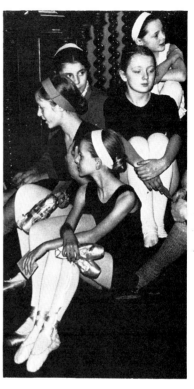

The students mentally rehearse their performances in unaccustomed reflective silence before being ushered into the examination room. Once inside they must perform in turn the set exercises laid down for each of the examination stages and their performance is appraised by an expert panel.

School
Performance

So my first year at ballet school progressed,
and how I enjoyed it! At the end of term
before we broke up for the summer holi-
days a very special event took place, the
school performance. Ballet schools all over
the world put on these productions as not only are they
great fun for students and teachers but they form an
important part of the background training of a dancer.
Everything involved in putting on a production was done

by the students themselves and with the help of our teachers we learnt about make-up, costume and scenery making, stage lighting, stage management, rehearsal and music. Most important of all, however, is that at the end of the preparation work most of us had our first taste of how it feels to perform before a live audience. I say most of us because some lucky students already had the good fortune to have been chosen for a children's part in a season's touring by one of the big ballet companies. I will never forget my first feeling of stage fright, nor how quickly it vanished when my cue came to go on stage. A great feeling of joy came over me as I began to dance and I knew that I had made the right choice all that time ago after seeing my first ballet.

Right: The Bush Davies School director gives a group of girls some useful advice at the dress rehearsal in the Adeline Genée Theatre.

Centre: It is essential for the student to be knowledgeable of all that has to be done in order to achieve a successful production. One of the girls gets practical experience with stage lighting cues.

Far right: Make-up is an essential art that all dancers are taught to master. There won't always be someone to do it for you.

Below: A scene from a lavish Royal Ballet School production of The Sleeping Beauty.

The beautiful dancer Suzanne Farrell demonstrates the fantastic elevation that she has become famous for.

Useful Information

he age at which a dancer begins to specialise is an important consideration. Girls need to start regular lessons by the age of nine, boys by about twelve.

There are today a number of schools in Great Britain which provide a general education up to G.C.E. level together with specialised dance training, so that both parts of a dancer's education can be under one roof, without any waste of time and energy in travelling between day school and dance teacher. Among these schools, the Royal Ballet School and the Rambert Ballet School are devoted primarily to classical ballet and there is no point in going to either school unless you really want to join a ballet or dance company. A lot of the other schools, however, offer other forms of dancing and also drama training in order to equip their students for a career in any branch of the theatre. Among the principal schools of this kind are:

The Associated Arts School, 61 Ridgway Place, London SW19

Stella Mann School of Dancing, 343a Finchley Road, London NW3

Brooking School of Ballet and General Education, 110 Marylebone High Street, London SW1

The Arts Educational Trust, Golden Lane House, Golden Lane, London EC1

The Arts Educational Trust, Boarding School, Tring Park, Tring

Bush Davies Schools (Residential), Charters Towers, East Grinstead, Sussex

Elmhurst Ballet School (Boarding School for Girls), Heathcote Road, Camberley, Surrey

Hammond School, 12 Liverpool Road, Chester

Legat School, Goudhurst, Tunbridge Wells, Kent

Anthorne School, 19 Quaker's Lane, Potters Bar, Herts

Northern Dance Centre, Lamberts Holt, Kirby, Malham, Skipton, Yorkshire

The legendary Margot Fonteyn in the role of the ballerina doll from Petrouchka.

Auditions for the Royal Ballet School are held regularly and they are very thorough. Particulars of entry can be obtained from the secretary, 155 Talgarth Road, London W14. There is strong competition for places and the school has to decide to the best of its ability which candidates are most likely to fully develop as ballet dancers. The school would obviously not accept those who are going to grow too tall, or those who have some physical defect, not necessarily apparent and not necessarily an impediment to normal living, that will prevent them from achieving success in classical ballet.

Scholarships

How can I get a scholarship? Does the Royal Ballet School give scholarships? Is there a lot of money involved in becoming a dancer? These are some of the questions frequently asked by students and their parents.

If you have a problem or do not know where to start,

Above: Marcia Haydee and members of the Stuttgart Ballet performing in "Innere Not". This is a modern ballet providing simple yet stunning decor.

Right: Maurice Bejart's Ballet of the Twentieth Century performing "Clown of God", a beautiful ballet telling the story of the great dancer Nijinsky.

Modern ballet still requires the dancer to have the technique of a classical training. Classical and modern ballet need the same skill and expression of movement.

Left: Boris Akimov as the mighty Roman general Crassus, hailing his troops in the Bolshoi production of "Spartacus".

Below: Mikhail Baryshnikov, truly a legend in his own time, effortlessly lifts Patricia McBride of the New York City Ballet in a scene from the Jerome Robbins work, "Other Dances".

you should in the first place get in touch with your Local Education Authority. Very many L.E.A.s will give grants for further study if they are convinced that the student is talented and the money will be well spent.

But most teachers know when and how to enter their pupils for scholarships. There are a number of scholarships available, but the Royal Ballet School itself can afford to give away very few (and those mostly for boys).

Then there are a number of scholarships given by the dance organisations. These are advertised well in advance in 'The Dancing Times', and the secretaries of the various bodies will always be glad to tell you what is available. If you have a particular school in mind, you should write to the secretary and ask if there are any special scholarships available.

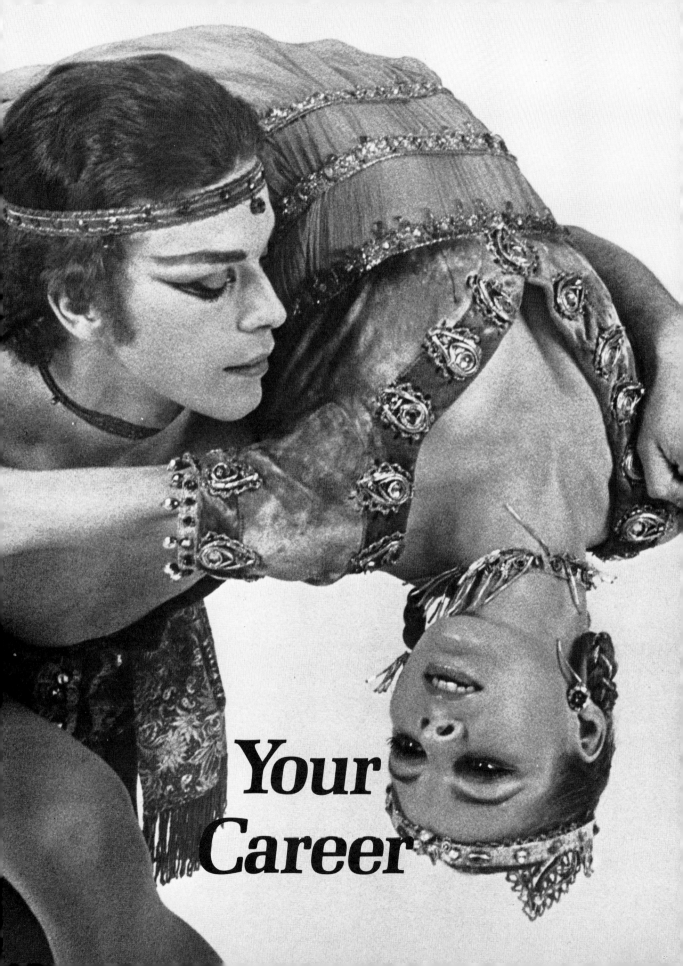

Your
Career

Graduates of the Royal Ballet School and of the Rambert School of Ballet have a good chance of being offered a job with the parent company. Dancers graduating from the other major schools are usually helped through their first audition and into their first job with the guidance of their experienced teachers.

There are always times and situations, however, when you will have to set about getting a job on your own. Application to the ballet master of any company is the first step, with a request to audition for possible vacancies. Most ballet masters will look at an ambitious dancer and if there is no vacancy with the company at that moment, it is possible that they will keep you in mind for a vacancy arising in the future.

In Great Britain, there are a number of ballet companies large and small. The large ones are what most dancers set their sights on, but a few years in a small company will provide you with important experience.

There are many opportunities in the German opera houses, every one of which has a ballet company of some kind. Many of these houses are able to employ dancers from overseas and some of the German companies do interesting and exciting work. The principal ones are in Hanover, Stuttgart, Berlin, Munich, Cologne and Wuppertal, but there are countless others.

Australian, South African and Canadian dancers who have trained abroad are now able, if they wish, to try for the national companies in their own countries.

Outside ballet, there are many opportunities for stage and television work. These jobs are filled, as a rule, from auditions, all of which are advertised in the weekly

The Prima Ballerina of the La Scala Milan company is Liliana Cosi, pictured here in the role of the wicked black swan Odile from "Swan Lake".

Left: Many of the young students of the Arts Educational, as seen here, have gone not only into ballet, but have made brilliant careers for themselves in all fields of entertainment.

Far left: Antoinette Sibley and Anthony Dowell in "Thais", a ballet created especially for them by Sir Frederick Ashton.

The radiant Lesley Collier dances the role of Princess Aurora in the Rose Adagio from "Sleeping Beauty".

newspaper 'The Stage'. Golden advice for auditions is to be immaculately groomed, simply but well made up, and practice clothes spotless. Always remember to take your different kinds of shoe so that you can do ballet, tap or modern as required.

If you grow too tall for ballet you can have an interesting and lucrative career with such dance troupes as those of Miss Bluebell and Monsieur Charley, both based in Paris. These organisations set a high standard and provide various opportunities for further training. They send dance troupes to all parts of the world.

If you decide, towards the end of your training, that you would rather teach than perform, you can take excellent training courses either at the Royal Academy of Dancing Teachers' Training Course or at the London College of Dance and Drama, administered by the Imperial Society of Teachers of Dancing. The Royal Ballet School offers a special Craftsman's Course for dancers who want to teach.

ell, that's how I started my dancing career and so far I'm loving every minute of it. Although the work is very hard and demanding and I sometimes feel like giving up when I find it difficult to get something just right, my love of dancing always carries me through and I dream of the day when I too may join one of the great international ballet companies and tour the world with them. Who knows, I might even become a star myself eventually and perhaps a young ballet student will have my picture as a pin-up on her bedroom wall! After all, nothing is impossible and I know that I am going to do my very best to achieve my ambition.

In the meantime, all I can do is practise very hard and dream of the beautiful ballets that I would love to dance in and some of the great dancers that I admire so much.

I hope that my story of life as a ballet student will encourage you and that you have enjoyed reading about it. Who knows, maybe one day you and I will be dancing in the same ballet!

Students at the Paris Opera school demonstrate perfect line in "Posé arabesque sur pointe".